SPLISHES an SPLO

Illustrated by Johnston and Cory

Nonsense Alphabet

A was once an apple pie,
Pidy,
Widy,
Tidy,
Pidy,
Nice insidy,
Apple-pie!

C was once a little cake,
Caky,
Baky,
Maky,
Caky,
Taky caky,
Little cake!

B was once a little bear,
Beary,
Wary,
Hairy,
Beary,
Taky cary,
Little bear!

Edward Lear

Something About Me

There's something about me
  That I'm knowing.
There's something about me
  That isn't showing.

  I'm growing!

Spider

I saw a little spider
with the smartest spider head:
she made — somewhere inside her —
a magic silken thread.

I saw her sliding down it.
She dangled in the air.
I saw her climbing up it
and pulling up each stair.

Aileen Fisher

Galoshes

Susie's galoshes
Make splishes and sploshes
And slooshes and sloshes,
As Susie steps slowly
Along in the slush.

They stamp and they tramp
On the ice and concrete,
They get stuck in the muck and the mud;
But Susie likes much best to hear

The slippery slush
As it slooshes and sloshes
And splishes and sploshes
All round her galoshes!

Rhoda W. Bacmeister

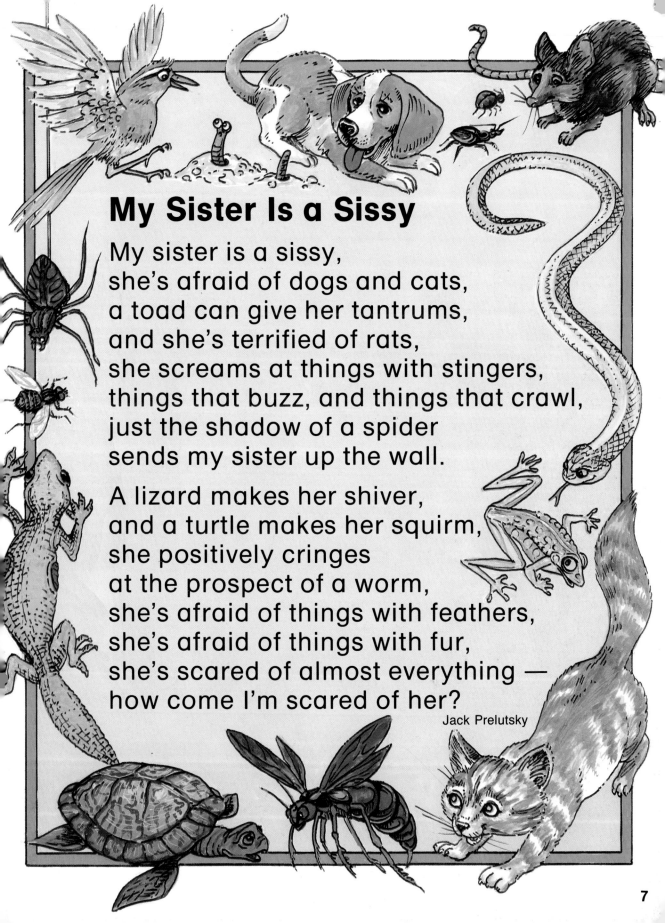

My Sister Is a Sissy

My sister is a sissy,
she's afraid of dogs and cats,
a toad can give her tantrums,
and she's terrified of rats,
she screams at things with stingers,
things that buzz, and things that crawl,
just the shadow of a spider
sends my sister up the wall.

A lizard makes her shiver,
and a turtle makes her squirm,
she positively cringes
at the prospect of a worm,
she's afraid of things with feathers,
she's afraid of things with fur,
she's scared of almost everything —
how come I'm scared of her?

Jack Prelutsky

The Witch on a Windy Night

An old witch sat at home all alone,
Cooking and cooking a big soup bone.
And the wind blew all around the house.

Shuuuuuuuuuu!

"Oh, who will share my soup?" she crowed.
"If I drink it all, I'll surely explode!"
And the wind blew all around the house.

Shuuuuuuuuuu!

A big dog barked at her front door.
"Go away!" she said. "I chased you before!"
And the wind blew all around the house.

Shuuuuuuuuuu!

"Oh, will you share your soup with me?"
The black cat purred, "With me? With me?"
And the wind blew all around the house.
Shuuuuuuuuuu!

"I've changed my mind! I hate to share!
"Let everyone starve for all I care!"
And the wind blew all around the house.
Shuuuuuuuuuu!

"I'll drink the soup myself!" she sang.
What happened then? She exploded. Bang!
And the wind blew all around the house.
Shuuuuuuuuuu!

Bernice Wells Carlson

Little Charlie Chipmunk

Little Charlie Chipmunk was a *talker.* Mercy me!
He chattered after breakfast and he chattered
 after tea!
He chattered to his father and he chattered to
 his mother!
He chattered to his sister and he chattered to
 his brother!
He chattered till his family was almost driven
 wild!
Oh, little Charlie Chipmunk was a very tiresome
 child!

Helen Cowles LeCron

I've Got an Itch

I've got an itch, a wretched itch,
no other itch could match it,
it itches in the one spot which
I cannot reach, to scratch it.

J. Prelutsky

Little Bird

One little bird with lovely feathers blue
Sat beside another one.
Then there were two.
Two little birds singing in the tree.
Another came to join them.
Then there were three.
Three little birds, wishing there were more:
Along came another bird.
Then there were four.
Four little birds, glad to be alive,
Found a lonely friend.
Then there were five.
Five little birds just as happy as can be,
Five little birds singing songs for you and me.

Mice

I think mice
Are rather nice.

Their tails are long,
Their faces small,
They haven't any
Chins at all.
Their ears are pink,
Their teeth are white,
They run about
The house at night.
They nibble things
They shouldn't touch
And no one seems
To like them much.

But / think mice
Are nice.

Rose Fyleman

13

When It Comes to Bugs

I like crawlers,
I like creepers,
hoppers, jumpers,
fliers, leapers,
walkers, stalkers,
chirpers, peepers...

I wonder why
my mother thinks
that finders can't be keepers.

Aileen Fisher

Grizzly Bear

If you ever, ever, ever meet a grizzly bear,
You must never, never, never ask him where
He is going,
Or what he is doing;
For if you ever, ever dare
To stop a grizzly bear,
You will never meet another grizzly bear.

Mary Austin

Rain, Rain, Go Away

Rain, rain, go away,
Come again another day,
Little Johnny wants to play.
Rain, rain, go to Spain,
Never show your face again.

Grace, Grace

Grace, Grace, dressed in lace,
Went upstairs to powder her face.

Two, Four, Six, Eight

Two, four, six, eight.
Meet me at the garden gate.
If I'm late, don't wait.
Two, four, six, eight.

I Eat My Peas with Honey

I eat my peas with honey,
I've done it all my life,
It makes the peas taste funny,
But it keeps them on my knife.

Ice

When it is the winter time
I run up the street
And I make the ice laugh
With my little feet —
"Crickle, crackle, crickle
Crrreeet, crrreeet, crrreeet."

Dorothy Aldis

Sakes Alive!

Sakes alive!
It's almost five!
It's time to have my dinner.
The outer part of me is fine,
But what about my inner?

Arnold Lobel

Nine Mice

Nine mice on tiny tricycles
went riding on the ice,
they rode in spite of warning signs,
they rode despite advice.

The signs were right, the ice was thin,
in half a trice, the mice fell in,
and from their chins down to their toes,
those mice entirely froze.

Nine mindless mice, who paid the price,
are thawing slowly by the ice,
still sitting on their tricycles
... nine white and shiny *micicles!*

Blow, Wind, Blow!

Blow, wind, blow!
And go, mill, go!
That the miller may grind his corn;
That the baker may take it,
And into bread make it,
And bring us a loaf in the morn.

I Was Going To Sell My Eggs

As I was going to sell my eggs,
I met a man with bandy legs,
Bandy legs and crooked toes,
I tripped up his heels,
And he fell on his nose!

Little Lamb

I heard a little lamb cry, Baa!
Says I, "So you have lost mamma?
    Aah!"

The little lamb, as I said so,
Frisking about the fields did go,
And, frisking, trod upon my toe —
    "Oh!"

23

Old Man of Peru

There was an old man of Peru
Who dreamed he was eating his shoe.
He woke in the night
In a terrible fright,
And found it was perfectly true.